We Are Light

– A Journey of Transformation –

Narim Bright

We Are Light

First edition: 2026
ISBN: 978-1-7644008-1-7

Narim Bright

The one who rekindled the fading light within me

was sent from heaven—

my hope.

Prologue

That night again, I was engulfed in chaos.

"Why on earth are you doing this! What do you expect me to do?"

My little daughter, whining late into the night without falling asleep, pushed me to my limit.

"Just sleep! Go to sleep!"

She cried even louder.

Unable to hold back any longer, I pushed her hard as she sat on the mattress in the dark room with the lights off. The little girl, who had been crying so loudly, suddenly fell silent, as if startled. A heavy stillness filled the room.

I called my husband to take over and stepped outside alone. Late into the night, I wandered aimlessly through the night.

'Why is this so hard for me? Why can't I be the person I promised myself I would be?'

That miserable routine kept repeating itself. Either I argued with my husband, or I felt overwhelmed by my daughter—sometimes both. During the time when COVID broke out and we had to spend most of our days confined at home, I realized that it wasn't just them who wouldn't go as I wished, but myself as well.

When I returned home, I made sure they were asleep, then went into an empty room alone and wrote in my journal. It was the only way I knew how to find my way when I felt lost. The pages were soaked with tears, the ink blurred and smeared. That was how frustrated and suffocated I felt. It was as if I were trapped in an endless tunnel. I wanted to escape this repetitive life.

In that moment, as I wrote in my journal, I realized that I had to choose.

There were four options:

To simply continue living day by day like this.

To walk away—leaving my husband and daughter behind.

To give up on life.

And finally,

To change.

Table of Contents

Part 6.

The Future Longed For

This book is my attempt to understand how real transformation happens.

It was born from personal pain, questions about time and consciousness, and a deep desire to stop passing pain to the next generation.

My perspective is influenced by Christian faith, scientific curiosity, and personal experience. I do not claim to have all the answers, but I hope these reflections help others find light in their own darkness.

Narim Bright

Part 1.

A Shift in the Observer

A Shift in Perspective

In the 16th century, the astronomer Nicolaus Copernicus introduced a new idea. Before that, people believed that the Earth was the center of the universe. They thought the sun, the moon, and countless stars all revolved around the Earth.

This belief wasn't just imagination. Humans observe the world from the surface of the Earth. When we look up at the sky, the sun and stars really do seem to move around us. So it made perfect sense to think that the Earth was at the center.

But when you shift your point of view beyond the Earth, a completely different picture appears. The Earth is not the center of the universe—it is simply one planet orbiting the sun. Even when looking at the same reality, what you see can change entirely depending on where you're looking from.

Our understanding of time is similar.

We tend to feel that time flows at a constant, steady rate—something absolute. We think of it as a kind of background that ticks along in seconds, minutes, and hours. But modern physics tells us that time can actually vary depending on the observer.

Albert Einstein's theory of relativity starts from a simple idea: the speed of light is the same for all observers. From this comes a surprising conclusion—time and space can change depending on the observer's state.

As an object moves faster, time for that object passes more slowly compared to the outside world. This is called "time dilation." In theory, as something gets closer to the speed of light, time slows down more and more.

This challenges one of our most basic assumptions:

Time may not be absolute.

Just as Copernicus changed how we think about the center of the universe, Einstein changed how we think about time.

Then, is the moment we're experiencing right now really just the present?

If Light Were the Observer

There's something we've been overlooking. Up to now, we've always talked about time from a human point of view—just like people in the past tried to understand the universe while standing on Earth and looking up at the sky. From a human perspective, time can only appear relative.

So let's shift our perspective once more.

What if the observer weren't us, but light itself?

Or what if we looked at time from the perspective of the entire universe?

Earlier, we saw that according to relativity, as an observer's speed approaches the speed of light, time slows down, and distances in the direction of motion shrink. If we imagine taking this to the extreme—reaching the speed of light—then time would approach zero, and distance would shrink to zero as well.

Of course, in physics, light itself can't be an observer. Because light has no proper time of its own. But as a thought experiment, imagining the world from light's perspective reveals something fascinating.

Suppose light travels from event A to event B. From a human point of view, there can be a vast distance and a long stretch of time between the two. For example, light traveling from a star billions of light-years away appears to take billions of years to reach Earth.

But from the perspective of light, the story is completely different. For light, there is no time interval between events. Along light's path, the "proper time" between A and B is zero. So from light's point of view, A and B are not separate events—they can be seen as a single event.

In this kind of thought experiment, if light were to perceive the world, it would not see differences between objects moving at different speeds, but instead encounter a world in which the very notion of time between events disappears. The process of movement and the flow of duration would no longer appear in the way we understand them.

As a result, from the perspective of light, even traveling across vast distances may appear as a single instant. What we understand as a sequence of events unfolding over time becomes a single moment.

This shows that the flow of time we experience is not absolute—it depends on the observer.

And when the observer is light, all events collapse into a single moment.

Seeing the Past

When we look up at the night sky, it feels like we're seeing the stars as they are right now. But in reality, we're not seeing their present—we're seeing their past.

Take Sirius, one of the brightest stars visible from Earth. It's about 8.6 light-years away. The light we see from Sirius today has been traveling through space for about 8 years before reaching our eyes. What we're seeing is not Sirius as it is now, but as it was about 8 years ago.

Another bright star, Canopus, is about 310 light-years away. The light we see from it began its journey roughly 310 years ago. So again, we're not seeing its present—we're seeing a version of it from centuries in the past.

When we look at the night sky, we're not seeing a single moment in time. We're seeing many different moments from the past all at once. Some stars appear as they were a few years ago, others as they were hundreds of years ago, and more distant ones show us light from thousands—or even millions—of years in the past. The night sky is, in a sense, a collection of different pasts gathered into one view.

So, in the universe, observation is always an act of looking into the past.

It takes time for light to travel from an event to reach the observer. No matter what we look at, we are not seeing its present, but a version that has already passed. This structure appears throughout the entire universe. If we were to look at Earth from a distant planet, the Earth we see would not be its present form, but a version from long ago. From that perspective, the "present self" becomes someone who already belongs to the past.

From this cosmic perspective, we are always standing in two positions at once. We are observers, looking at other things—but from somewhere else, we are also objects being observed, already part of the past. In one frame, we are living in the present. In another, we already exist as history.

So, observation has a common structure: the observer is always positioned after the event, and what is observed always appears as the past. This is the fundamental way we perceive the world on a large scale.

But there is one more essential condition. For any observation to happen, something must carry the information from the object to the observer.

That something is light.

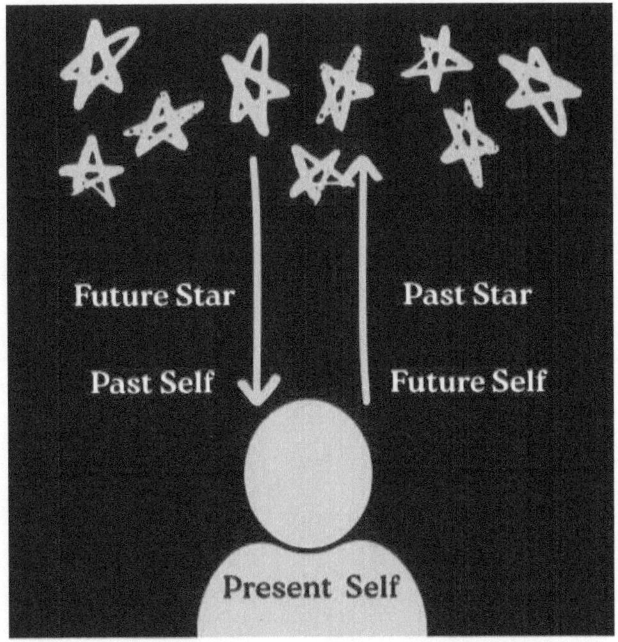

Why We Are Able to See

Light that leaves a star travels across vast stretches of time before reaching us, and through that light we are able to see the distant universe. This reveals an important point: the reason we can observe the universe at all is because of light. Without light, objects might exist, but they would not appear to us. Light does more than simply illuminate—it serves as the channel through which the world becomes visible.

If the external world is revealed through light, then through what is our inner world revealed?

Even with our eyes closed, we can still bring scenes to mind. We see landscapes in dreams, recall someone's face in thought, and imagine things that have not yet happened. In that realm, there is no external light entering from outside—and yet, we are still clearly seeing something.

This fact points to an intriguing possibility: that the inner world of humans also has its own way of being revealed. Just as objects in the external world are disclosed through light—their colors and forms becoming visible—there may also be a medium within us through which thoughts, memories, and imagination are revealed.

We tend to overlook this because we are so accustomed to relying on physical light. And we think without even being aware that we are thinking. Yet when we turn toward the inner world, we are still seeing and sensing it from a place of perception that is not bound to the physical eyes. From that inner standpoint, we are able to see and experience things without the need for external light.

Now, let us turn our attention to the inner world.

Part 2.

Light and the Light of Consciousness

Light Where There Is No Light

At the time, my little daughter loved the color green. Every night, she would fall asleep holding a green toy in her hand. One night, after the lights were off and she and I were lying in bed, she suddenly realized she hadn't brought her green toy with her.

"Green! Green!"

It meant she wanted it right away. On many nights before, I would turn the lights back on, go out to the living room, find the toy, and bring it back to her. But that night, I was completely exhausted. I didn't want to get up, and I didn't want to turn the lights on again.

So I said to her,

"Green? Look—everything is black right now. Without light, there is no green. In the morning, it will be green again."

She was quiet for a moment, then accepted what I said. And after that night, she never looked for her green toy in the dark again.

We usually think that objects have color, but in reality, color is not a property that exists on its own. It only appears when light is present and reflected in a certain way. The moment light disappears, green, red—every color disappears with it. Anything that does not emit light becomes black in the dark.

And yet, even when we close our eyes and block out all external light, we can still see something. In dreams and in thought, there is no external light, but we clearly experience images—and even other senses.

This suggests something important: there is also light within that realm.

The Outward Man, The Inward Man, The Light of Consciousness

Human beings have the ability to move beyond space and time through thought. We tend to take this for granted, but it is, in fact, an extraordinary ability. Within our thoughts, we can do anything. Unlike the physical world, this inner space is free from external constraints—it is a realm that belongs entirely to each of us.

This ability is also one of the key traits that distinguishes humans from other living beings. Animals rely on past experience and memory to respond to situations, but humans are not limited to what they have experienced. We can imagine possibilities that do not yet exist, create entirely new worlds in our minds, and bring them into reality. Much of the physical world we live in today began as someone's thought. Houses and cities, technology and art, civilizations and systems—all of these started in the mind of someone. Thought is not just something that passes through the mind, but the starting point of creation itself.

For this reason, human existence is often described as consisting of "body, mind, and spirit." Here, to deepen our understanding, we can describe it in another way: "the outward man, the inward man, and the light of consciousness".

The outward man refers to the physical body that exists in the material world. It changes over time and grows old—a being bound to the flow of time.

The inward man exists in the inner realm of thoughts, emotions, and the mind. It is where meaning is formed freely, beyond the limits of space and time.

And there is a deeper layer still—the light of consciousness, which illuminates all of it.

The outward man ages with time. But the inward man can be renewed again and again. At the center of this transformation is the light of consciousness.

"For which cause we faint not; but though our outward man perish, yet the inward man is renewed day by day."

— 2 Corinthians 4:16 (KJV)

"Take heed therefore that the light which is in thee be not darkness."

— Luke 11:35 (KJV)

Three Kinds of Light

We live within three kinds of light: the external light that reveals the outer world, the inner light through which our inner world appears, and the light of consciousness that illuminates even the unconscious aspects of our being.

On Earth, the natural sources of light that illuminate the external world are the sun, the moon, and the stars (setting aside artificial light). Through them, we are able to see. During the day, we see objects by the light of the sun. At night, we see faintly by the moonlight—which reflects the sun— and by starlight. When day returns, the brightness of the sun overwhelms the stars, and they disappear from view. In this sense, the true sources of light in the external world are the sun and the stars, the luminous bodies.

Now let's turn to what appears within us.

We can see our thoughts. Thoughts themselves act as a kind of inner light. In this sense, thoughts are like stars. Even when we are not paying attention to them, stars are always present in the night sky. In the same way, thoughts arise on their own, without effort. We cannot touch them, but we can see them. To think deliberately is like choosing to look at a particular star in the night sky. This way of understanding reveals something important: thoughts are not identical to who we are—they are something we can observe, like objects appearing before us.

And beyond this, there is another light—the light of consciousness.

This light is like the sun. When we consciously observe a thought that has arisen unconsciously, it can disappear in an instant—just as stars fade from view in the brightness of daylight. Shining the "sunlight" of consciousness onto the "starlight" of thought is what it means to become aware of unconscious processes.

At the same time, the light of consciousness reveals truth. When a thought is not merely a fleeting distraction, but a sudden insight, bringing it into conscious awareness makes it clearer and more vivid. Just as sunlight reveals the world around us, the light of consciousness reveals what is true.

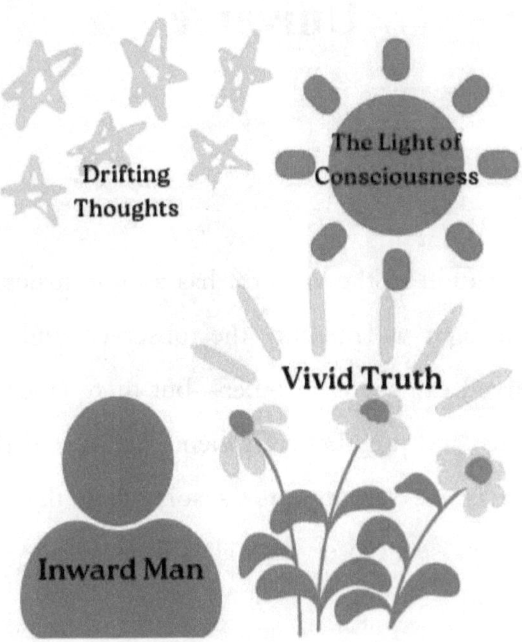

Drifting Thoughts
The Light of Consciousness
Vivid Truth
Inward Man

The Inward Man in the Universe

Observation in the universe has a clear structure. When light is present, the observer and the observed can see each other—but there is always distance and time between them. Because of this, whatever we see appears as something that has already passed. Observation always takes place after the event.

Interestingly, a similar structure appears within our inner world. Just as we can see things in the universe through light but cannot touch them, there is also something within us that we can see but cannot physically grasp. This is the realm of the inward man.

Just as the outward man lives in the physical world, the inward man lives in the inner world. While the outward man moves through everyday life, the inward man is constantly moving through thoughts, choosing what to focus on from moment to moment.

At some point, the inward man focuses on a single thought. In that moment, the thought becomes something being observed—and at the same time, it becomes something that has already passed. It doesn't matter whether it's a memory of the past, an imagination of the future, or even a thought about the present. The moment it is observed, it has already become something past. The "I" who is observing always stands after the thought. I am in a position ahead of the thought, looking back at it— as if from the future.

But in the world of thought, observation doesn't work in just one direction. The moment we observe a thought, that thought also begins to reflect us. Within the thought, I am not only the observer—I also become something that appears within it.

Then the thought becomes a possibility of the future, while the "me" in the present becomes something that has already passed.

So, in the world of the inward man, thought can be both past and future, and reality itself can also be both past and future. Different moments in time exist together within a single relationship.

And the time in which all of this happens is always now.

Mere thought

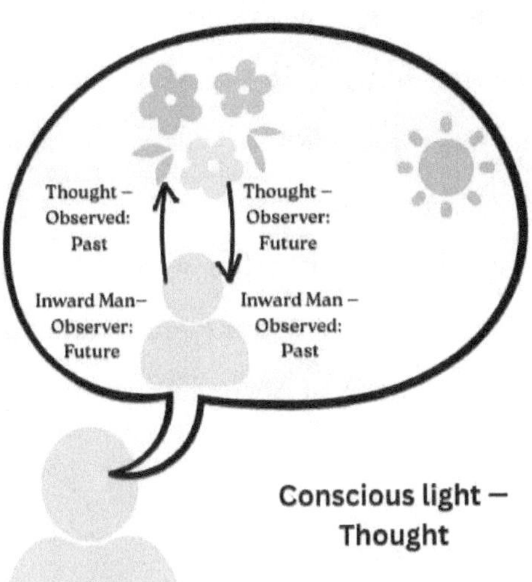

**Conscious light —
Thought**

Imagining the Future?

Let's say you're going to cook something. First, you think about what you want to make and what ingredients you'll need. You picture the whole scene in your mind. Only after that do you begin to act. Even if your plan changes along the way, those changes also happen first in your thoughts. In moments like this, we usually say that we are "imagining the future." It seems as if our present self is looking ahead at a future event in the mind.

But if we look at this from a broader, almost "cosmic" perspective, this situation can also be understood as a form of observation.

The moment you picture a scene in your mind, that thought becomes something you are observing. And the moment it becomes an object of observation, it is already something that has, in a sense, passed.

Thus, thinking becomes an act of looking at events that are already in the past. Conversely, the "I" who is observing those thoughts is positioned after those events. I stand as a future possibility, looking back at the events within my thoughts.

So, imagining the future is not merely about creating something that does not yet exist; rather, it can be understood as a process of looking at events that have already become past and drawing them back into reality.

Remembering the Past?

Then how does recalling the past work?

When we recall the past, we tend to think we are simply bringing back events that have already happened. The past and the future may appear to be directions of time moving apart, but in the realm of thought they actually share the same structure of observation. Because, wherever there is light, the observer and the observed can switch places.

The moment we observe an event in thought, it no longer remains merely as a past event. That scene itself can become a kind of observer, capable of looking at the present self. At that point, what we consider the past turns into a possibility for the future.

In other words, the past, present, and future are not fixed. This is why we often repeat presents and futures that resemble the past: past events look at who we are now, and that gaze, in turn, guides our choices and actions in the time to come.

In the end, whether we are imagining the future or recalling the past, thinking itself is the act of observing something that has already appeared—something that is, in a sense, already past. And depending on how we look at it, or which scenes we choose to focus on, our decisions, our actions, and even the direction of our lives can change.

The past we "see" is not simply what happened—it is a version we interpret and choose, sometimes selecting or even reconstructing it ourselves. Although past events have already passed, depending on what we choose to believe among those events and how we view them, they can unfold in directions entirely different from their original nature in thought. Memory can be distorted. Even the same event is remembered differently by different people. And yet, we still tend to accept the past as a fixed fact, treating it as something that cannot be changed.

Then why do we cling so strongly to such a changeable past?

Moreover, why do we so persistently hold on to certain events, even if they continue to trouble us in the present?

Part 3.

The Place of the Observer

The Existence of the Observer

We usually regard the thoughts that arise in us and the self as the same being. We say that they are mine, my thoughts, my self. However, with just a little attention, we come to realize that we are beings capable of standing apart from thought.

The reason is simple: we are able to observe thoughts.

Whether we are recalling a memory or imagining a scene, we are able to look at it. That means a thought is not who we are—it is something we can observe. It is something outside our being.

Thoughts continually appear and disappear. Depending on one's will, some thoughts linger for a while, some are not let go of, and others keep arising. In a single day, countless thoughts appear and disappear within the inward man's environment. Yet the one who observes these thoughts does not disappear. Thoughts may fade, but the one who is able to observe them does not. In this sense, our inward man is truth.

When this observer is awake, we are no longer carried away by our thoughts. We can notice a thought, choose whether to engage with it, and sometimes let it go. But when we are unaware of our presence as the observer, we can no longer distinguish between ourselves and our thoughts. We get swept along by them, speaking and acting as they lead us. In that state, thoughts become our identity.

So, what truly matters in understanding our inner world is not simply what thoughts arise. It is whether we are able to observe our thoughts and to understand where those thoughts originate.

And at that point, we come face to face with yet another layer of our inner world:

The background through which the "stars" of thought arise—

the subconscious, which forms the environment of the inward man.

The Inward Man and the Subconscious

Human beings are given two remarkable gifts: thought and emotion.

Thought is the source of our creative power, and emotion is what enriches our experience of life. To truly understand and work with these, we need to understand the environment in which the inward man lives—the subconscious.

As a human being experiences life and the body grows, the subconscious is formed. The subconscious is the environment in which the inward man lives, its background. It is much like how there exists a material environment in which the outward man, the physical body, lives.

Before we become aware of the subconscious, the inward man tends to live centered around the outward man. At this stage, most of our thoughts and emotions are driven by past experiences. We interpret the world and respond to it based on what has already been stored within us. In this sense, our way of living is not so different from that of animals.

During this phase, it is not easy to move toward new possibilities. Even if we know that a better life is possible, we tend to remain within what is familiar. Because we respond unconsciously based on past experiences, it becomes difficult to manage our thoughts, emotions, words, and actions. So, our present choices and future direction are strongly shaped by the past.

Just as we need to know where we are living in order to decide whether to stay or move, we also need to recognize the state of our subconscious. If we want to change our lives, we must first begin by reshaping this inner environment. It is like moving to a better place. From a change in the subconscious, we can begin to shape both our present and our future.

When we come to understand the subconscious and begin to renew it, we often describe this as "waking up" or being "born again." From that moment on, we are able to observe ourselves consciously and respond with awareness.

That Day at the Playground

How deeply the subconscious influences our thoughts and actions can be seen even in the smallest moments of daily life. I came to realize this clearly after becoming a mother.

When I was pregnant, I made a firm promise to myself: "I will never lay a hand on my child. I will never discipline my child out of emotion. And I will never fight with my husband in front of my child." I was determined never to cause my child suffering, either mentally or physically.

However, that promise did not endure. I found myself caught in repeated conflicts with my husband, and there were moments when my child no longer felt purely lovable. It was as if I were trapped deep within a dark, endless tunnel. No matter how desperately I struggled, I could not move forward—I remained where I was.

One day, I took my ten-month-old daughter to the playground. The ground was covered with soft bark chips. She crouched down, playing with them, then picked one up and brought it to her mouth.

"Hey! What are you doing? That's dirty! No!"

In that moment, I didn't even realize how on edge my emotions were—I reacted automatically, as if it were the most natural thing. But the startled, flustered look on her face told me everything: how intensely emotional I had been. As if to show me, she put another piece into her mouth again.

Seriously?

"Fine, then eat them all! Eat everything here and get a stomachache! I'm leaving!"

I turned away and left her there alone. Then I hid behind a tree on the outskirts of the playground and watched her. She stayed there, still squatting, without moving.

What could that tiny little girl have been thinking in that moment?

As I looked at her small figure from behind, a thought suddenly hit me—what was I doing as a mother? A wave of guilt and regret rushed over me. I went back to her, and we returned home together.

While she was taking a nap, I sat alone and thought deeply.

'Why did such a small act leave me so unsettled, so sharply on edge? It was a completely natural behavior for a toddler at her stage of development.'

'How can I actually live the way I promised myself I would?'

'How can I become a gentle, kind mother?'

Then, suddenly, memories from my own childhood came to mind.

My grown-ups argued frequently. Discipline was often driven more by emotion than by clear principles, and it felt like walking on eggshells every day. (I don't mean to blame them. There were times when I did, of course. But now, understanding that they also went through difficult childhoods, I feel compassion for them. And without their dedication, I wouldn't be who I am today.)

The scenes I experienced repeatedly as a child settled into my subconscious, shaping me as though they were part of who I am. I never consciously chose them, yet I found myself carrying the same kinds of words, behaviors, emotions, and values.

I wanted to stop that cycle here. I didn't want to pass it on any further.

So early one quiet morning, I went into an empty room and sat alone. I brought back memories of moments when I had made someone uncomfortable—like what happened at the playground. What had happened when I behaved like my daughter did as a child? In my memories, I saw the same patterns—anxiety and anger. Just recalling those moments made my body tense and my heart race.

I took a deep breath and looked at those memories again—but this time, differently. I reimagined them the way I truly wished they had been. I pictured grown-ups who accepted my clumsy behavior with love, who guided me gently and kindly.

As I began to see my past memories in a new light, a completely different set of emotions rose up within me. It felt as if a part of me that had been stuck in a dark tunnel had finally seen the light outside. In that moment, I broke down in tears. It felt like all the pain and emotions that had built up inside me for so long were finally being released and washed away. After embracing this new, peaceful version of my past, nothing seemed to trigger me anymore—no pain, no lingering hurt, no trace left behind.

After that, I also revisited the moment at the playground with my daughter.

When she picked up a piece of bark and tried to put it in her mouth, I reimagined how I would respond. This time, I saw myself calmly and gently telling her that it wasn't something to eat. It wasn't a serious situation—I didn't need to react so strongly. Then we would go play on the swings together. I pictured it as a peaceful, ordinary moment that both of us could enjoy.

That image became a possibility—a future waiting to appear in reality.

A few days later, I went to the same playground with my daughter. Just as before, she seemed to check my reaction and then brought a piece of bark into her mouth again. It was exactly what I expected. Situations that trigger me tend to come back again and again—until I understand the cause and change it. In a way, it feels like a second chance, as if life is giving me another opportunity to begin again. Another reason is that I had already imagined it, so it showed up as a new possibility for the future.

This time, something was different. Because I had already shifted something in my subconscious by rethinking it, I didn't feel angry. I responded calmly, gently—even playfully—telling her it wasn't for eating. Then she smiled. After that, we spent a peaceful time together, playing on the swings and the slide.

Just like the scene I had already created in my mind. Because I had already rehearsed it internally, putting it into action didn't feel difficult at all.

A Double-Edged Sword

We use our thoughts to make sense of our experiences and to find direction in life. Our thoughts shape how we see reality, and they can also help us discover new possibilities.

However, because thoughts are so powerful, they can also work against us. Some thoughts deepen our understanding, while others create misunderstanding and bias. Some help us see reality more clearly, while others pull us away from it. When used well, our thoughts can guide us; if not, they can turn into a maze. If we don't stay focused on objective reality and instead spend too much time in our subjective thoughts, we can easily become lost in illusions and distorted perceptions. That's why thoughts can be a double-edged sword.

To truly understand life, we need balance between the inner and outer aspects of our being. While the outward man lives through real experiences in the world, the inward man searches for meaning within. When these two reflect each other and come into harmony, life begins to take on clear direction.

At the center of this balance is the light of consciousness—and it must remain awake.

The light of consciousness helps us recognize what we are truly perceiving. It shows us whether we are moving in the right direction toward our destination, or losing our way in illusion.

Life finds its meaning and direction when the outward man, the inward man, and the light of consciousness come together to fully live in the present moment.

Being Fully Present

Consciousness is the eye of the inward man. (In this sense, the light of consciousness is like the sunlight in the inner world.) There are moments when consciousness becomes fully focused on a single object—we call this state a state of flow.

In our daily lives, our consciousness constantly moves back and forth between reality and our thoughts. Then, in moments of deep focus, that scattered awareness settles fully on a single direction, a single object.

The noise of our thoughts quiets down, and we become fully present in the moment. In that state, we lose track of time, and our whole being exists completely in the here and now.

The nature of deep focus can be divided into two types, depending on where our consciousness is directed.

When our consciousness is focused on physical activity or sensory experience, we become deeply immersed in reality. Whether we are absorbed in our work, fully focused on studying, engaged in exercise, or concentrating on our breath in practice, we begin to experience an inner stillness as our thoughts quiet down. In these moments, our whole being becomes fully immersed in the reality of the outward man, because the outward man and the inward man are both directed toward the same place.

On the other hand, when our consciousness turns inward, we become immersed in the inner world of the inward man. We may smile or feel tense as we watch scenes in our mind, and even without any physical stimulus, our bodies can still experience sensations and respond as hormones are released. During prayer or meditation, people naturally close their eyes and reduce external input—to become fully absorbed within. By blocking the outward man's view, we are able to focus completely on the inward man's vision.

In this way, immersion arises when our consciousness is directed toward a single point. It shapes our emotions, our actions, and ultimately the direction of our lives.

However, like anything else, it isn't always positive. Being in a state of flow doesn't always lead us in a good direction—what matters is what we choose to focus on.

The Direction of Flow

Immersion—what we often experience as a state of flow—can be divided into two types: flow toward the light and flow toward the dark, depending on the hormonal changes and the direction of our emotions at the time.

In light-oriented immersion—what we might call a positive state of flow—there is a sense of peace and gratitude. There is also a refreshing kind of joy that is hard to put into words. We experience this kind of deep absorption when we are moved by a powerful book, fully engaged in exercise, immersed in meaningful work, listening to beautiful music, or taking in the beauty of nature.

This kind of immersion also arises within the inner world of the inward man. Through deep reflection, prayer, meditation, or inner practice, we enter a state of deep inner focus. In those moments, the light of consciousness becomes clearer, and our whole being experiences a sense of stillness, peace, and quiet inner joy.

This kind of immersion helps us grow and enriches our lives. It can bring new insights and reveal meanings we hadn't seen before. That's why moments of deep focus often lead us to rediscover direction in life.

On the other hand, there are times when immersion leaves behind emptiness or turns into something difficult to control. This is immersion in darkness. Examples include addiction to drugs, pornography, or escapist fantasies, or harmful obsessions.

This kind of immersion also arises from deep focus—but instead of setting us free, it gradually takes control of us. It may begin with intense stimulation or pleasure, but over time it becomes addictive, making it harder and harder to break away, until a person becomes a slave to it.

In those moments, the light of consciousness grows dim, and we lose the ability to see ourselves clearly. We become disconnected from the direction of that light. That is why it is called immersion in darkness.

When someone is deeply immersed, there is one way to tell whether their focus is directed toward light or darkness: just look into their eyes. The look in their eyes reveals where their consciousness is directed. The reason people's eyes feel so different is because of what they are usually immersed in—whether they tend to enter states of light or states of darkness.

Part 4.

The Beginning of Change

The Inheritance of the Subconscious

I really hated being nagged by the grown-ups when I was a kid. If something they had put away wasn't exactly where it should be, I'd get in trouble. Same thing if I didn't wipe down the bathroom after a shower. If I accidentally broke a dish, the first thing I did was check their reaction. If anything didn't sit right with them, I'd get scolded. There wasn't much patience for me to learn or grow out of my mistakes. They would either hold it in for a bit—or suddenly snap.

But then I began to see those same patterns show up again in a place that didn't feel unfamiliar at all— in the way I treated my spouse and my daughter.

I had always believed that once I got married, I would become the kind of wife anyone would admire—wise, gentle, and beautiful. But reality turned out differently. Small things started to get to me—clothes left on the floor, socks on the table, and all the chores piling up.

I found myself repeating the same things over and over, irritated by everything. Before I knew it, I had become someone who nags. And the words coming out of my mouth sounded exactly like the ones that had bothered me so much as a child.

"I'm so sick of this!"

"How many times do I have to tell you?"

"When are you going to learn?"

I was sure I wanted to live differently. I had wanted so badly to leave behind a home filled with blame and constant nagging—so why was I living the same way? I didn't want to keep living like this. And I didn't want this way of life to be passed on to my daughter.

So how could I change? How could I stop the emotions, words, and reactions that seemed to come out automatically? I wanted to find a way.

As I was trying to figure out how to change, I noticed something interesting. We like to think we're choosing how we respond, but most of the time, we're just reacting out of patterns built from repeated experiences and memories. The things we went through over and over again in childhood quietly settled within us, becoming our default way of responding. So instead of choosing something new, I kept falling back into the same patterns.

That's when it clicked. If repeated experiences shaped who I am now, then I could also change by building new ones. I started to believe that I could change—that I could have more peaceful relationships, love people the way I truly wanted to, and become the person I wanted to be.

And it all had to start with taking an honest look at what was already inside me.

Reality Shaped by Belief

In psychology, there's a concept called 'Learned Helplessness'.

To control a young, untrained elephant, a trainer ties a chain around its leg. No matter how hard the elephant struggles, it can't break free. After going through this over and over again, it eventually learns:

"I can't break this chain."

But as time passes and the elephant grows into an adult, things are different. It's strong enough to pull a tree out by its roots. And yet, it still doesn't try to break the chain—not because it can't, but because it believes it can't.

A similar pattern appears in human psychology in many different ways. One example is the 'Self-Fulfilling Prophecy'. When we believe that something will happen, we tend to act in ways that align with that belief—and in the end, that belief becomes reality.

"I'm not good at relationships."

With this belief, a person becomes cautious in every interaction and keeps a distance from others. As a result, their relationships actually grow more distant. Then they say again:

"See? I knew I wasn't good at relationships."

Other beliefs take the form of 'Limiting Beliefs'.

"I'm bad with numbers."

"I'm not the kind of person who should speak up."

These beliefs are not proven facts—they are conclusions. But over time, they begin to function like part of a person's identity.

What all of these ideas have in common is this:

What binds us is not reality itself, but the conclusions we have already formed about reality. That's why even when circumstances change, our behavior often does not. Even when we gain strength, we don't try. Even when opportunities appear, we don't take them.

We tend to think that reality is what's holding us back, but in truth, it's our beliefs about reality that keep us stuck.

The Beginning of Change

The thoughts that arise and the words and actions that come out automatically are mostly rooted in the subconscious. Earlier, we described the subconscious as the environment in which the inward man lives. And at the center of that environment is one key element: belief.

Belief is not just a religious idea. Most of our everyday choices are also based on what we believe. What we believe to be possible or impossible shapes the choices we make next. And most of these beliefs are formed through our past experiences.

To understand this, let's return to the example of the elephant.

As a young elephant, it is tied with a chain. No matter how hard it tries, it cannot break free. After repeated failures, it reaches a conclusion:

"I can't break this chain."

As time passes, the elephant grows stronger. It now has the power to uproot a tree. But it still doesn't try to break the chain—not because it lacks strength, but because it believes it can't. A conclusion formed in the past continues to control its actions in the present.

Then one day, the elephant notices a herd of other elephants—running freely across a wide, open plain.

In that moment, two thoughts arise:

'I can't live like that.'

'I want to live like that.'

The difference between these two thoughts comes down to one thing: Hope for what we truly want.

And so, change begins with hope.

The elephant that begins to hope looks again at the chain that binds it. It recognizes that the chain is what stands between itself and freedom. But at the same time, memories from the past resurface—the failed attempts, the disappointment, the frustration. Those feelings begin to rise again.

Even so, the elephant no longer wants to live that way. The desire for something different becomes deeply strong.

So, the elephant begins to imagine a new scene— one where it breaks the chain around its leg and runs freely across the open field. Instead of holding onto conclusions formed by past experience, it starts to focus on a new possibility.

And in that moment, the next step of change emerges: Action.

An action it has never truly attempted before: Breaking the chain.

"For as the body without the spirit is dead, so faith without works is dead also."

— James 2:26 (KJV)

Restored by Truth

For a long time, I struggled. I couldn't stay present, and my emotions would easily take over. It was hard for me to stick with any job, and my relationships with family and friends weren't very fulfilling. I often went through long periods of despair, but on the outside, I acted like everything was fine.

Even after I found faith, even after I got married, my life didn't really change. Being a mom felt overwhelming and exhausting. The arguments with my husband never seemed to stop. I lived like I was on autopilot, reacting automatically like a programmed robot. Even small things would trigger strong emotions, and I couldn't seem to stop it. It felt like my inward man was always standing in the middle of a battlefield—barely holding on, constantly on edge, never knowing when the next attack would come.

I didn't like who I was. I didn't like the life I was living.

Then, at one point, I realized something that marked a new beginning. My inner world was deeply connected to my past experiences. What I was feeling now wasn't just about the present—it had already been shaped by old memories and experiences.

From that moment on, I began to trace my emotions back, like putting together pieces of a puzzle. I looked for the memories behind the feelings I was experiencing, connecting similar situations that brought up similar emotions. As I followed those patterns, I started to uncover their roots. Memories from childhood, familiar and repeated experiences—even the ones I couldn't clearly remember—began to surface from my subconscious.

Then I asked myself, What was it that I truly wanted back then? And I knew the answer clearly. What I longed for wasn't to be looked down on just because I was a child, but to be respected. Not criticism, but encouragement. Not fear, but love.

So I began the work of looking at those moments again—this time in a different way.

I imagined a family where people understand and love one another, a place where even the young and vulnerable are treated with respect. Not discipline driven by emotion, but guidance shaped by clear standards and fairness—where right and wrong can be learned in a healthy way. That was the kind of family, the kind of world, I truly longed for as a child.

Looking back at my past in this way turned out to be simpler than I expected. And it made the changes I wanted to see in myself feel more within reach. But most people find it hard to accept that this can be a key to resolving their present struggles. We tend to believe the past is fixed and unchangeable, and so we go on repeating the same patterns in our present and future.

I was no different. Then at some point, I found myself deeply longing for change—for a life that felt free and at peace. It was for my daughter, but it was also for myself.

I am certain of this: the people who hurt me in the past did not act out of their true intentions. They, too, were responding from their own memories, experiences, and subconscious patterns—just as there were moments when I hurt my own daughter without meaning to. In that sense, they, too, were not free.

And yet, we are not without hope. We have the chance to write a new story—because wherever there is light, time is always now.

The moment we begin to see our past in a new way, we take the first step toward changing our past, our present, and our future.

And that step can begin right now.

Part 5.

New Pasts

Changing the Past

Why do similar problems keep repeating in our lives? And why do we find it so difficult to control them?

We keep bringing past experiences and emotions—ones we don't even want—into the present. Even if the people involved change, if the situation follows a similar pattern, the emotions from that time remain alive and continue to repeat themselves in our present lives. The past itself is gone, but the memories and feelings tied to it are still alive in our subconscious.

It's hard for us to control these reactions because they don't happen consciously—they happen automatically. Much of this automatic processing is tied to the brain's fast, habitual systems and to the autonomic nervous system, which regulates our body's responses. Because of this, our emotions and reactions can be triggered much more quickly than we expect. We may find ourselves repeating responses we don't want, while feeling unable to stop them.

Rather than trying to fix things on the surface, we need to identify the root cause of the problem first. We need to change it so that past experiences no longer operate as present problems. We replace the emotional patterns and reactions shaped by unwanted past experiences with new experiences and new meaning.

But this naturally leads to a question:

Can we really change the past?

How can we possibly change something that has already happened?

We tend to think of our present self as something built from our past. Who we are now is the result of accumulated thoughts, words, and actions over time, or something we were simply born with. Because of this, changing ourselves can feel almost impossible—like trying to change our own DNA.

However, when we begin to understand our experience of time from both a macro and a micro perspective—and recognize that all change begins within our inner world—the story starts to shift.

As we've seen, the inner world doesn't follow time in the same way the physical world does. In reality, building a house takes time and effort. But in our thoughts, we can build a house instantly and experience ourselves living in it. Even though it's not physical, we can still imagine the feel of the sofa, or picture the view outside the window.

In the same way, while we can't return to the past in real life, within our inner world we can revisit the past at any time—and even shape it as we wish.

Memory itself exists within us, so when the memory changes, the past changes with it. Because the inward man is not bound to one point in time—it can exist in the past, present, and future, all from the standpoint of now.

So change can happen much faster—and it starts first—within our inner world.

We can't scoop up spilled water and put it back, but we can pour it out completely and fill the container with fresh water. In the same way, we may not be able to change or erase what happened in the past, but we can reshape how we carry it within us.

That's where this journey really began—figuring it out together, through light and time.

The Memory of That Day

There was a memory inside me—a wound that had been left to fester for a long time. There were probably many, but I'll share one of them. It no longer controls me as an unconscious belief, but even now, when I think back on it, my heart still aches.

I was fourteen when it happened. I was a good student and usually did well in school. But one day, my exam results didn't turn out the way I'd hoped. When I got home, the grown-ups were having dinner. I was afraid they'd be disappointed with my test results, and I was already upset about it. So without even realizing it, I slammed my door and went straight into my room without saying hello.

Then all of a sudden, one of the grown-ups came into my room. Without any explanation, the beating started. I was beaten all over—kicked and struck with a stick. There was no real reason for it. Maybe it was because I had slammed the door.

Backed into a corner, I was being beaten hard, hearing words I can hardly repeat—along with this:

"I've done everything I could for you! There's nothing more I can do! You're so ungrateful!"

Even now, as I write this, it still hurts.

All I wanted was to do well. I wanted to get good grades and make them proud. But going through adolescence wasn't easy for me either. I wanted the grown-ups I loved to understand me. I wanted them to tell me that exams weren't everything in life—that it was okay even if I didn't do well. But that day, instead of understanding, I was met with violence.

Looking back now, maybe that grown-up couldn't help it either. They were living with wounds inside that they didn't know how to deal with. Unhealed pain can stay with a person for a long time. I was carrying those scars too, along with many others.

I sometimes wonder if anyone could truly understand how long I had been stuck in that tunnel. Of course, I know there are many people who have gone through even more than I have.

There was a time when I could hardly stand the sound of a baby crying. As my daughter grew and began to express her emotions, I felt the urge to lash out at her more times than I can count. I didn't want to pass my pain on to her—I had promised myself again and again that I would never lay a hand on my child.

But that promise felt almost meaningless. No matter how much I wanted to be a good mother, my emotions, my words, and my actions wouldn't follow my will. It felt like I was being controlled by something I couldn't see—I couldn't control myself. I felt completely defeated.

I cried and prayed on my own every day. I wanted to know how I could keep from passing my pain on to this small, fragile child. So I started writing letters to God each day, almost like keeping a journal.

Then one day, I finally received an answer.

A Move in the Subconscious

Now, we begin the process of changing the painful memories that remain in the subconscious. This is often called "cleansing the unconscious" or "healing inner wounds," but I like to describe it as "Relocating the Subconscious of the Inward Man." It is the process of revisiting painful childhood memories and seeing them in a new way—so that we are no longer bound by them, but instead move our inner environment to a new place.

Through this process, I was able to break free from patterns I didn't want and begin living my present and future in the way I truly desired. This was the very first step—more important than anything else—in creating real change in my life.

I've always been sensitive and easily affected by my emotions, and the memories of past wounds stored in my subconscious made it hard for me to handle what I was feeling in the present. That tendency shaped the direction of my life in ways I didn't even realize at the time. In the end, it took me a long time to reach and maintain the sense of peace I truly wanted.

Before we begin this process of "relocating" the subconscious, there's something we need to recognize clearly.

First, when we look back on our days, there have been far more moments of care and love than moments of hurt. Just being able to breathe, eat, drink, and rest means we've already been living within countless moments of care. And yet, memories of pain tend to be deeply imprinted within us and linger for a long time. They can become magnified inside us, making even a brief moment feel as if it lasted forever.

Second, many people who hurt others are often acting from wounds they have never healed. They, too, wanted to give love. But they were reacting from their own unhealed wounds. In the end, it was their unprocessed subconscious patterns that shaped how they acted.

The process of seeing those painful memories in a new way is actually quite simple. We return to those moments and see them again—not as they were, but as we truly needed them to be.

This is possible because what we observe becomes our past. When we keep looking at painful memories, we lock them in place and keep bringing them into the present, reliving the same pain again and again. But if we choose to look at those memories differently—right now—then the past begins to shift.

So, I revisited that day like this:

But one day, my exam results didn't turn out the way I'd hoped. My steps on the way home felt heavy. I was disappointed in myself, and the thought of the grown-ups being even more disappointed weighed on me. So without even thinking, I slammed my door and went straight into my room.

My grown-ups waited quietly, giving me space until I calmed down.

In my room, I listened to music I liked and slowly found a sense of peace. Before long, I fell asleep. When I woke up hungry, I walked into the kitchen. On the table was a meal prepared with foods I liked. Next to it was a small note.

My dearest girl,

It seems like something happened at school today.

Was it because your exam didn't go well?

In life, there are times when things go well and times when they don't.

It's okay.

If something else made your heart heavy, let's let that go too.

I am always proud of you, and I'm so thankful you are my daughter.

Enjoy your meal.

I love you.

I went back to that day and saw it again the way I had wished it had been.

Then I cried and cried—as if my inward man were being washed clean through those tears, as if I were being baptized and born again.

Releasing the Inner Waste

One of the biggest benefits of revisiting our memories in a new way is this: instead of reacting automatically, we're given a brief moment to pause, think, and choose consciously.

Even after I reshaped those painful memories the way I wanted, I didn't suddenly become a consistently gentle, loving mother. I still needed to practice speaking and acting as this new version of myself. And inside me, there were still all the uncomfortable emotions, harsh words, and traces of violence I had carried for so long—piled up like trash.

It almost felt like my daughter could see all the mess that had built up inside me. She kept triggering it, over and over again. With her bright, shining eyes, that small and fragile child felt like a messenger sent from heaven—an angel that felt almost like a little devil at times, sent to heal and clean out what was inside me.

When she whined, got stubborn, suddenly screamed, or even poured her milk out and dumped her cereal on the floor on purpose, something inside me would just flare up. In those moments, I would go straight to my room alone. I'd even turn up my daughter's favorite music so she wouldn't hear any of it. It was time for my own quiet ritual—letting out the mess that had built up inside me.

Once I got into my room, I'd grab a pillow or stuffed toy and physically release the anger I was carrying—away from my daughter, away from anyone else. I cried, screamed into a pillow, and let the intensity pass until I could return calm enough not to hurt anyone.

After letting it all out, I'd feel completely drained—like all my energy had been pulled out of me. But at the same time, something inside me would settle. Then I'd go back out like nothing had happened, clean everything up, and go back to being her mom.

This had to be done alone, somewhere no one could see or hear me—so I wouldn't take it out on anyone else and let that emotional "trash" settle into them. Sometimes it took five minutes, sometimes just one. I'd pour everything out into something inanimate—a stuffed toy, a plastic bottle, a piece of paper, a pillow—using it as a way to let everything out. Over time, I found myself needing to do it less and less. And now, no matter the situation, that intense red alert reaction no longer rises within me.

Since then, that painful memory from my past no longer drives me toward anger or emotional reactions. The past, now seen in a new way, a cleansed inner world, and consciously chosen responses in my words and actions—these have reshaped the environment of my subconscious.

Over time, that painful memory from my teenage years faded. It became just another scene from a movie—something that no longer had any hold on me.

The Moon Hidden Behind the Clouds

If uncomfortable emotions suddenly come up, it may be a sign that there's something from the past connected to that situation that needs to be addressed.

I used to get really frustrated whenever my daughter played with her food. When she made a mess at home or got loud in public, I could feel that uncomfortable reaction rise up in me. So I kept telling her to stop, over and over again. But of course, she didn't—because for a little kid, that's completely natural. She was only one or two at the time. I wanted to understand what was really going on.

One thing became clear—it was never really about her.

A child who grows up in a violent home can end up becoming a violent parent too—without even realizing it, even if they once swore they never would. A parent shaped by that environment often doesn't have the emotional space to calmly deal with a young child's behavior. The moment a child's actions bring up uncomfortable feelings, they may react automatically—often in the same way they were treated when they were young.

That reaction isn't so much intentional as it is automatic—like something that was programmed long ago being played out. Past experiences become a pattern of response, repeating themselves in the next generation. And before they even realize it, their own childhood gets passed on to their children.

That's what happens when the light of our consciousness is not awake.

We don't usually try to change the past. Since it's already happened, trying to change it can feel fake, forced, or unnatural. So even when we know something in the past hurt us, we hold onto it as we remember it.

And that's how the past keeps showing up in the present. We end up feeling the same emotions and reacting in the same ways, over and over again. When I stay stuck on a painful past, even ordinary situations can start to feel like problems—and before I know it, I turn them into problems.

But here's something we often miss: the events that once caused us so much pain aren't necessarily the truth themselves.

The people who hurt us were living in their own distorted version of reality, with the truth hidden from them. What they showed us wasn't who we truly were—it was the pain they carried inside. Just like there were moments when I, as a mother, made my daughter—whom I love more than anything—feel fear instead of love.

The truth was hidden, like the moon behind the clouds.

Perhaps, in the end, truth is deeply connected to love.

Unconditional love is the essence of who we are. So when we look at the past in a new way, we are not creating something false—we are uncovering the truth that was hidden.

We can reshape painful memories into the form we truly wished they had taken. And we can let go of the mess inside us without throwing it onto anyone else. It's like not leaving spoiled milk sitting in a cup, but pouring it out, washing the cup clean, and filling it again with fresh milk.

When we begin to see our memories this way, they no longer remain in the subconscious as intense emotional triggers. It feels as if we've been released from the chains that once held us. The tension within us softens, and a quiet peace settles in. The fear that once came from those wounds begins to heal and fade away.

Someone who helps heal others can see the traces of past wounds in their words, their actions, and the look in their eyes. So they offer the words that person once needed to hear, and respond with a gaze and actions rooted in love. That is what it means to set the past right.

This isn't something that can only be done by someone trained or especially loving. I can do this myself. In fact, I'm often the one best suited to do it—because no one knows my past better than I do, and no one understands what I truly needed more clearly than I do.

And this is possible because there's a light within us— a light that leads our whole being toward growth.

Practical Steps for Real-Life Application

The process of restoring past memories is not complicated.

Through the following steps, we can begin to see the past in a new way and change how we respond in the present.

---

1. Notice the pattern in the situation and your emotions

- Pay attention to moments when you overreact in certain situations.

- Ask yourself, "Why is this affecting me so strongly?"

- Don't judge—just observe the feeling as it is.

---

2. Acknowledge that your reaction is rooted in the past

- Understand that the issue isn't just the other person's behavior, but that something within you has been triggered.
- Recognize that past experiences, especially from childhood, can automatically shape how you feel now.
- Instead of blaming someone, be open to the possibility that this is a learned pattern passed down over time.

---

3. In a quiet space, revisit your younger self

- Bring to mind a specific childhood memory where you experienced something similar.

- Let yourself feel what you felt back then—the emotions and even the physical sensations (anxiety, tension, anger, a racing heart).

- Don't try to push the feelings away—just let them be and observe them.

---

4. Reimagine the memory the way you wish it had been

- In that scene, change how the grown-ups respond to your younger self.

- Replace criticism and fear with understanding and love.

- Let yourself fully feel the peace and love in that moment—really take it in.

5. Let the emotions release

- You might find yourself crying or feeling a strong emotional release.
- This is a natural part of the process—old, built-up tension is letting go, and healing is beginning.
- From this point on, your subconscious starts to shift.

6. Revisit a recent situation as well

- Bring to mind a recent moment where you felt triggered or uncomfortable.
- Reimagine that scene with the response and behavior you wish you had shown.

- This helps your mind and body get ready to respond differently when a similar situation comes up again.

---

7. When a similar situation comes up again, choose a new response

- Because you've already reshaped the memory, the old automatic reaction doesn't take over the same way.

- Instead, choose the emotion and response you truly want, and keep reinforcing it.

- Little by little, you begin to build a new inner environment within your subconscious.

---

8. When the "inner mess" starts to come up, release it in a healthy way

- When strong negative emotions rise and you feel like you might lash out—through harsh words or actions—step away to a safe place where you can be alone.

- Instead of suppressing it or taking it out on someone else, let those built-up feelings and reactions out in a safe way.

- Over time, the intensity of those emotional reactions starts to fade.

Painful memories from the past can be seen in a new way—right now. When the memory shifts, your reactions in the present begin to change. And as those new responses continue, your subconscious starts to change too.

Then you're able to respond the way you truly want to—living this moment with a sense of peace. In the end, your present and your future begin to change as well.

**** This book shares my personal journey of healing and transformation. Everyone's path is different, and some wounds may require additional support from trusted professionals, community, or loved ones.**

Part 6.

The Future Longed For

Life Is BCD

There is a saying: "Life is BCD." It means that between Birth and Death, there is Choice. Life is a continuous series of choices.

In the inner world, thoughts are always rising—like stars in the sky. Some shine more brightly when illuminated by awareness, while others fade away.

"Which one will be held onto?"

At any given moment, we choose one of them. And when that choice turns into words and actions, the thought gains strength.

We shape who we become through what we think, say, and do. As our choices are repeated, they begin to turn into beliefs—and those beliefs settle into the subconscious. Over time, that subconscious starts to drive our thoughts, words, and actions automatically, shaping the direction of our lives. And the more we repeat the same choices, the more our lives move in that direction.

Thankfully, we can adjust our direction and become the person we want to be. Now, this process can be guided intentionally. Through conscious choice and repeated practice, new patterns of thought and action can be planted into life. As this continues, new beliefs take root in the subconscious of the inward man. Eventually, those beliefs begin to express themselves naturally in everyday life.

Ultimately, change is not something forced through effort, but something formed through repeated choices.

Life is the result of choice.

And even now, in this very moment, a choice is being made about how to live.

We Come from the Future

As we've already explored, what we see with our physical eyes is actually the past we experience as the present—because light takes time to reach us. Everything we see has already happened. The moment we realize this, the way we see life begins to change.

The observer always stands after the event. To observe something means to be positioned beyond it in time. In that sense, what feels like the present can be seen as something that has already passed.

When we start to see things this way, we no longer react automatically to what happens. Instead, we're able to take a step back and watch life as it unfolds. We can fully feel what's good, and let go of what isn't without holding onto it. Life no longer drags us along—we begin to move with its rhythm and experience it more deeply. Almost as if we're looking at the past from somewhere in the future.

So far, we've been living by looking at the present through the lens of our past experiences. But now, we can begin to see life from a different place—from the version of ourselves we want to become. From that place, even what's happening now becomes something that has already passed. And instead of being driven by fear of the unknown, we can choose how we respond to the present with a deeper understanding—like looking back on something we've already lived through.

At that point, we no longer react based on old patterns. Even if the world around us looks the same, something within us has already changed.

Someone who has come from the future already understands much more. So they're not easily shaken by what happens in front of them. They experience life as if they're looking back on something that has already passed.

"Yeah… that was really hard back then."

And this way of living is available now.

In this very moment, it is possible to think, choose, speak, and act from the place of the self that is already aligned with the desired future. And those choices begin to shape life in that direction.

There is no longer a need to remain in a present shaped by the past.

We can live this moment through the light of consciousness from the future we truly want.

A Better Self

A few years ago, I misunderstood a friend, and it led to a small conflict. I misread her intentions and sent a long, emotional message. At the time, it didn't feel like a misunderstanding—it felt like I was right. But in the end, it was a big mistake. Even the friends who heard it said it was my fault. In the end, I apologized to her.

If I had been more aware in that moment, what would I have done differently? I probably would have noticed that I was misunderstanding her. I would have taken a step back from my thoughts and emotions and looked at the situation more clearly. If I had done that, I might have seen where it was leading before sending that long message— and I wouldn't have reacted or acted on impulse.

So what about now? Do I always make better choices? Do I no longer react on impulse? Not really. The same kinds of situations and problems keep showing up, helping smooth out the rough edges in me. Even now, there's still a lot I'm not fully aware of—things that need to be corrected as I grow into a better version of myself. As long as I see them as "mine," I'll keep repeating the same patterns—until I realize they're not truly who I am. That's why the things we call problems in life keep coming back.

But something has changed. I'm able to notice my inner state and my reactions more often now. Of course, there are still moments when I react emotionally or on impulse. But I don't get discouraged, because I know those reactions can be changed. I can step back and observe my thoughts instead of being pulled along by them. I can choose how I speak and act—and practice it. And in that way, I've become freer than I used to be.

In relationships, what people often need from me isn't sharp advice or solutions—it's empathy, understanding, and acceptance first. That's what my friend needed from me, too.

I'm learning not to try to manipulate or change others anymore. I choose to respect their choices and accept them as they are—to see them and love them as they are.

At the same time, I choose who I want to be. I choose myself as someone who lives in love and peace. And instead of trying to fix others, I simply choose to change myself—for a better way forward.

"But he knoweth the way that I take: when he hath tried me, I shall come forth as gold."

— Job 23:10 (KJV)

The Mystery of Matter and Energy

One of the most remarkable abilities given to humanity—as children of a Creator—is the ability to create. And creation always begins with thought. What we repeatedly focus on often shapes our decisions, behaviors, and therefore the reality we experience. To understand this more deeply, we turn once again to Einstein's discovery.

Einstein showed through the principle of mass–energy equivalence—expressed in the formula $E = mc^2$—that matter and energy are deeply connected and can be transformed into one another under certain conditions. This discovery became the theoretical foundation for technologies like nuclear power, and it opened up a new way of understanding the world—not just as a collection of physical matter, but as something we can also understand in terms of energy.

In this equation, E stands for energy, m for mass, and c for the speed of light. The fact that mass is deeply connected to energy shows that the world we live in is not made up of solid matter alone, but is also closely connected to energy, even if we don't always notice it.

The emotions we feel can become powerful drivers. And the direction we keep our attention on often shapes the direction our lives move in. When we keep coming back to a certain possibility and repeatedly feel it as real, it starts to play out in our lives—through the way we think, speak, and act.

Even if our thoughts or emotions don't directly create physical matter, what we focus on and how we feel still shape our moment-to-moment choices.

Those choices influence the way we speak and act—and over time, they shape our reality as well. That's why so many self-development and success teachings point to the same direction.

Many people have experienced this in their own lives and shared what worked for them. But even when we hear their stories and try to follow the same steps, we don't always get the results we hoped for. Then we start to question the principle itself.

But maybe the issue isn't the principle. Maybe our current awareness is still shaped by the past, and we're not yet ready to fully take in something new.

That's why, if we want to apply this in our lives, two things really matter.

First, what we truly want must be aligned with our thoughts, emotions, words, and actions. If someone wants to lose weight but constantly thinks about food and overeats, the desired result will not follow. If someone wants success but takes no action, nothing will change.

Second is belief. It has to do with the state of our subconscious. No matter how positive or vivid the imagination, it doesn't easily show up in reality if doubt is still there inside. When what we want isn't aligned with what we truly believe, it tends to hold us back and block possibilities. In the end, it's belief that moves us into action.

"Will this really work? Can I really do this? See, it's not working."

But when a possibility is truly believed, that belief changes attitude and choice—and ultimately changes the direction of life. This is why we began our story with an understanding of light and time— to renew our sense of belief.

Where there is light, we can see. And life moves in the direction of what we look toward. The eyes of the inward man can perceive possibilities before the physical eyes can see them. And in time, the moment comes when those possibilities become visible in the physical world as well.

"Then touched he their eyes, saying, According to your faith be it unto you."
— Matthew 9:29 (KJV)

"Now faith is the substance of things hoped for, the evidence of things not seen."
— Hebrews 11:1 (KJV)

We Are Light

We can go anywhere in our minds and imagine anything. That is a remarkable ability we've been given. The moment we become aware of it, we begin to see time differently. The past, present, and future are not completely separate—they all exist within this single moment we call now.

Memory brings the past into the present, and imagination brings the future into the present. That's why the past, present, and future are all experienced within this moment. This is how we experience time.

When we look toward the future with the eyes of the inward man, that future already exists in a sense— it's already present in our awareness. And through our choices and actions, it gradually takes shape in the outer world. In the end, what we call the present reflects what we've seen inwardly and chosen repeatedly through thought, word, and action.

So in this very moment, we have a choice. We can renew our subconscious, become aware of our automatic patterns, and begin to live from the future we truly desire. By seeing time differently, the past can be reshaped and the future can be chosen—because we are not just observers of the world, but beings that carry the light through which it is seen.

Up to this point, we've explored different ideas and perspectives to rethink our understanding of time. But in the end, there is one simple reason we are able to live all of time in this present moment:

Light has no time.

For light, every moment is now.

Where there is light, all time is now.

To see is to know that light is present. And to see even with our eyes closed is to realize that there is light within us.

In the end, every moment and every experience exists now.

And so, we are light.

"You are the light of the world. A city that is set on an hill cannot be hid.

Neither do men light a candle, and put it under a bushel, but on a candlestick; and it giveth light unto all that are in the house.

Let your light so shine before men, that they may see your good works, and glorify your Father which is in heaven."
— *Matthew 5:14–16 (KJV)*

Light shines brightest in the darkness.

Perhaps the dark seasons of life

exist so the light within you

may shine even brighter.

And one day—

your light will surely shine.